THE LITTLE BOOK OF
RAYBURN
TIPS

THE LITTLE BOOK OF
RAYBURN
TIPS

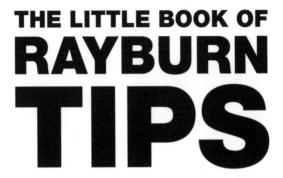

RICHARD MAGGS

Absolute Press

First published in Great Britain in 2003 by
Absolute Press
Scarborough House, 29 James Street West
Bath BA1 2BT, England
Phone 44 (0) 1225 316013 **Fax** 44 (0) 1225 445836
E-mail info@absolutepress.co.uk
Web www.absolutepress.co.uk

A catalogue record of this book is available
from the British Library

ISBN 1 904573 10 X

Printed and bound in Italy by Lego Print

'All that you say in your advertising about a Rayburn is true. It does cook better. It does give lashings of hot water, and it does keep the kitchen warm and dry. But you leave out so many of the small advantages that busy housewives appreciate.'

Mrs Reading of Eynsford, Kent
From an unsolicited testimonial first published in the *Rayburn Cookery Book*, 1958

Place an **orange** or **lemon** in the main oven for several minutes, depending on temperature, before squeezing to **extract the most juice.** Organic citrus fruits give a far superior flavour and are worth the extra cost.

For **toast that doesn't stick,** the hotplate must be at a medium temperature – cook directly on the hotplate in the middle or use the simmering end.

Toasted sandwiches

work well here too, allow 3-4 minutes each side.

Leave **jars of jam** or syrup for 30 minutes on the top plate of the Rayburn, with their lids loosened, **to soften** for easy spreading when baking. Runny **honey** and golden syrup, which have become crystallised, may be similarly rendered **clear again.**

Stale white bread will make

wonderful dried breadcrumbs.

Discard all the crusts and blitz them in a food processor, then dry out on a tray on the top of the cooker overnight.

To clean your Rayburn

use Aga-Rayburn cleaning paste. Rub it on all over the enamel and leave it for a good five to ten minutes. Then wipe it off along with all the dirt. But don't use it on chrome lids – a soapy cloth and dry towel are best here.

To loosen tight metal screw-top jars,

simply place the lid side down on the simmering end of the hotplate for 30 seconds. The metal lid expands and then is easily twisted off using a cloth.

Make **fat-free croûtons** for garnishing soups and salads by dicing bread and crisping in a cool oven. Leftover cooked bacon pieces can be cut up and finally crisped in a cool oven to make delicious bacon bites for garnishing salads.

To dry out **wet shoes,** football boots and trainers, hang them over the Rayburn rail by tying their laces together.

Dry awkward-shaped metal cooking **utensils** and kitchen gadgets, graters, and the like, on the warm top plate so they don't go rusty in storage.

Use the gentle warmth of the top of the Rayburn to **soften, melt or warm** ingredients for cooking. Soften butter, melt chocolate and warm bread flour in the bowl for brilliant bread making.

If you have an open fire, **dry out kindling** for it in a cool Rayburn oven. With a solid fuel Rayburn rapid lighting will now always be possible. Be creative – dried out orange peel makes excellent tinder!

Keep your hotplate free of toast crumbs
and the like, by brushing with an
Aga-Rayburn wire brush.

An absolutely
clean hotplate

is essential to ensure efficient heat transfer
to saucepans.

When drying **sheets,** duvet covers and jeans with your Rayburn, turn after a couple of hours and they **will scarcely need ironing.** Make sure that the air vents for the burner are not covered up.

13

Discover the joy of

Agalinks,

Aga-Rayburn's very own Internet lifestyle portal.
Point your browser to www.agalinks.com for
the very latest owners' news and content,
including the cooking and kitchen section.

When **baking bread** throw an ice cube onto the floor of the oven just before shutting the oven door. The cube will melt and the steam produced will ensure **a perfect crust.**

Always keep your plain shelf cold

and stored away from the Rayburn. This can then be placed on runners above any food which is browning too quickly in the oven. It must be cold to have this shielding effect.

Seal the freshly cut ends of **nylon cord** and rope for gardening and boating needs. Twist the fibres to a point and dab on the boiling end of a hot hotplate to fuse the ends **to prevent fraying.**

Always place your

Aga kettle on the Rayburn

hotplate with a slight twisting action to ensure
perfect contact. To boil efficiently keep free from
scale. To ensure continued peak performance,
get into the habit of regularly descaling your
kettle with an approved product.

18

Consider installing an old-fashioned overhead pulley clothes airer, which can be used

for drying washing overnight.

Alternatively, use an A-frame airer or old-fashioned clotheshorse for drying washing in front of the Rayburn. You will save a lot on tumble dryer running costs.

Dry out mushrooms and apple rings overnight

in a cool oven, but remember to leave the door ajar. First soak the peeled and sliced apple rings in acidulated water for 5 minutes to prevent them going brown. Make up using 2 teaspoons of Vitamin C powder per pint of warm water.

Everyday stock is really easy.

Place a chicken carcass in a pan along with a clean unpeeled and halved onion, some sliced carrot, together with a stick of celery if available and a few peppercorns. Cover with water and bring to a simmer on the hotplate and then place covered in the oven at a simmering temperature for several hours. Strain, cool and freeze.

When **planning your new kitchen,** try and fit in an airing space fitted with telescopic rails to the side of your Rayburn for hand and tea towels. This is also a good place to store the larger Rayburn oven accessories that won't fit in your kitchen cupboards.

If you keep poultry, dry your

used egg shells in a tin in a cool oven

and crush very finely before incorporating back into your fowls' diet to save buying fresh oyster shell.

23

Rayburn chef's pads

are great for protecting the insulating lids when you want to place something to warm on top. They also serve as

useful pot grabs.

Purchase a cheap

meat-roasting thermometer

in order to determine accurately when meat is cooked to the stage you like. This takes the guesswork out of testing and ensures that a thorough cook is achieved preventing any risk of food poisoning.

Fitting a rail on the wall or ceiling
above your Rayburn for hanging ironed

shirts to air, and wet jackets to dry,

can be a simple yet highly efficient laundry aid.

Demijohns of **wine will ferment well** in the nurturing warmth of the Rayburn. Leave on a work surface near to the cooker or, if you are a keen winemaker, designate an area next to the cooker for this purpose.

Clarify butter and

make your own ghee.

Place a pack of unsalted butter in a basin in a cool oven for 30 minutes. Remove and allow to cool a little. Skim off any foam, and pour off the clear ghee, discarding the milk solids left behind.

Children's paintings, collages and appliqué **masterpieces** will **quickly dry** out on a tray on a trivet on top of the hotplate lids.

A few inexpensive

cork mats
are invaluable

to protect the top plate, when using to warm
teapots and gravy boats, without scratching
the enamel.

Always rinse out a milk pan with cold water before using it to heat up milk on the hotplate. After use soak immediately in cold water. Both these tips

make washing-up much easier.

Bread dough will prove brilliantly if the bowl is

placed on a work surface next to the Rayburn. And for the final rise leave the bread tins on a trivet on the top plate.

Dry your own
herbs

by placing them overnight on cake cooling
racks on a trivet on top of the hotplate lids.
Once thoroughly dry, crumble and store in
clean airtight jars in a cool dark place.

Take the chill off

red wine from your cellar

by placing the opened bottle on a folded cloth
for a short while at the back of the Rayburn.
Be careful not to over-warm, however –
the term 'to chambré' was coined long before
central heating warmed our houses....

When **stir-frying**

with an Aga wok, preheat the empty wok on the simmering end of the hotplate for minute oe two before transferring to the boiling end ready for producing

a stylish
fast meal.

35

If you have **cereals that have lost their original crispness,** dry them out by spreading them on a tray in a cool oven for a few hours with the door slightly ajar. This also works for biscuits and crackers.

Bake-O-Glide

is a re-usable non-stick coated cooking material which lasts for years. Purchase a roll and cut up to customise your collection of bakeware and make preparing parchment linings a thing of the past.

The Aga cast sauté pan

is a brilliant all-purpose utensil. The ground base heats up rapidly, it fits in the ovens, and the high sides contain splatters. The lid converts it into a useful everyday casserole and with its enamelled exterior it is smart enough to send to table.

Dry stale bread scraps

to make rusks and filler for dog meal.
Break up into marble-sized pieces and leave
for several hours in a cool oven.

Keep a **wooden saltbox** or pottery **'salt pig'** near your Rayburn for **free-flowing dry salt** to season your cooking. I prefer Maldon salt or the French *fleur de sel*.

Home-made

granola-style breakfast cereals can easily

be made by drying out the well-tossed mix of oats, nuts, raisins, maple syrup etc, on trays in a cool oven.

Dry your
plain cast iron **pans** or exposed
cast iron ground bases in the warmth of
the Rayburn on the top plate
to prevent
rusting.

An Aga

cast iron trivet

is a good investment as it

protects
work surfaces

from hot dishes emerging from the ovens.
Your Aga kettle can also live on its own trivet
near the Rayburn ready for rapid boiling.

Once you have thoroughly cleaned

paintbrushes,

suspend them in a jam jar with elastic bands
and leave on the top plate to thoroughly

dry out without

the bristles becoming misshapen.

Irish
soda bread

is a great Rayburn store cupboard standby

for emergencies

– fantastic with home-made soup. Keep the
sieved dry ingredients ready-weighed out in
an airtight container or buy a mix ready-made.

Keep a mug of **coffee hot** whilst chatting on the phone by leaving it on the top plate. **Butter** may also be melted here ready to dress freshly **cooked vegetables** for an attractive finish before sending to table.

Make your own **golden breadcrumbs** by drying out stale white bread overnight in a cool oven. Blitz afterwards in a food processor.

Wipe up spills promptly as they happen with a damp cloth, especially with acidic liquids such as milk and fruit juice.

Clean as you go

is the key to keeping your Rayburn pristine.

Dry your own flowers

for attractive out of season arrangements

and to make pot-pourri.

Hang bunches over the Rayburn rail or place securely hooked on the wall above your cooker.

Heat a **terracotta tile** in a moderate oven for ten minutes. Then place in the base of your **breadbasket** under freshly baked or warmed rolls. Send to the table at the last minute and they will keep **warm** until required.

In the depths of winter, warm your hats,

scarves and mittens on the top of the Rayburn before braving the elements. Post-sledging clothing can also be quickly dried off on the Rayburn.

Acknowledgments

My thanks to all my family, friends, colleagues, fellow chefs and of course every Rayburn owner for their constant support and encouragement. To everyone at Aga-Rayburn; it is a pleasure to work with such an enthusiastic group of people. Also a huge thank you to my publisher, Jon Croft and editor and graphic designer, Matt Inwood at Absolute Press who are now great friends and Rayburn devotees.

Richard Maggs

A dynamic and accomplished chef, Richard is an authority on Aga and Rayburn cookery. As well as having featured on TV and radio, he has written for several food magazines, and contributes a regular column to the official Aga Magazine for Aga and Rayburn owners. He is also the resident Aga and Rayburn cookery expert, The Cookery Doctor, with the award-winning Agalinks website at www.agalinks.com.

His first book, *The Little Book of Aga Tips* turned him, overnight, into a bestselling author.

A selected list of Aga and Rayburn titles from Absolute Press

All titles are available to order. Send cheques, made payable to Absolute Press, or VISA/Mastercard details to Absolute Press, Scarborough House, 29 James Street West, Bath BA1 2BT. Phone 01225 316 013 for any further details.

Richard Maggs' *Aga Tips* titles
The bestselling Aga Tips series: indispensable for every Aga and Rayburn owner.

The Little Book of Aga Tips (2.99)
The Little Book of Aga Tips 2 (2.99)
The Little Book of Rayburn Tips (2.99)